Collections for Young Scholars™

Phonics Review

PROGRAM AUTHORS
Marilynn Jager Adams
Carl Bereiter
Jan Hirshberg
Valerie Anderson

CONSULTING AUTHORS
Michael Pressley
Marsha Roit
Iva Carruthers
Bill Pinkney

OPEN COURT PUBLISHING COMPANY
CHICAGO AND PERU, ILLINOIS

Cover art by Nelle Davis
Illustrated by Jack Wallen

Contents

Read all the words in the fish tank. Pick words to finish each sentence. Write the words on the blank lines.

1. We went to the zoo to see the fish. We went in Dad's new _____.

2. Dad _____ the car in the lot.

3. There were many _____ fish tanks at the zoo. They were bigger than my fish tank.

4. We saw a big _____ in one tank. It was swimming with the other fish.

5. Some fish can do tricks. Do you think sharks are _____?

6. I bet the fish do little all day. _____ says it must be _____ to live in a fish tank.

Name

Copy the sentence that tells about each picture.

1. There is a big barn on the farm.
   There is a big car in the park.

_____

2. It is dark in the park.
   There is a shark in the yard.

_____

3. Mary started to write a card.
   Mary's car will not start.

_____

4. The army was in the garden.
   The party was in the garden.

_____

5. The artist put large jars in his car.
   The artist put his brushes in a jar.

_____

Phonics Review

Read the story.

Thirty hens lived in a farmyard. Some hens were fat, some hens were thin. The fat hens giggled and made fun of the thin ones. The fat hens even had the dogs bark at them. One sunny morning in March, the farmer said, "I think I will have a party and fix several chickens in the oven."

Before it got dark, the farmer went out into the farmyard to get the chickens. The fat hens started to run as far as they could. But they were too fat to run fast. The farmer picked all the fat ones and left the thin ones alone. Then the thin hens giggled and were happy because no one made fun of them.

Now circle all the words that have the *ar* sound as in *star.* Then use some of the words in sentences of your own.

_____

_____

_____

_____

_____

_____

_____

_____

_____

_____

_____

Some things are missing from this picture. Read the
story. Then draw the things that are missing.

1. A girl lives on a farm. She is in the garden by the tree.
2. There are flowers in the garden.
3. A red bird is on top of the barn.
4. A bigger, yellow bird is on the left side of the fence.
5. A big, black dog barks at the bird that is sitting on the barn.
6. A farmer is by the barn. He has a basket of corn.
7. The farmer has a purple shirt. He also has a hurt arm.

Name

Pick words from the list to finish the sentences in the story below.

sisters   purple   church   turkey
nurses   summer   ferns   birds
together   curls   older   grandmother

June is my best friend. We go _____ to practice in the school band.

June lives next to the _____ with the bell tower on the corner.
There are many green _____ in her garden.

June has two younger _____ and one _____ brother.

June has dark, long _____. She has a pet turtle and two
_____. She loves the color _____. She also loves
_____ sandwiches. We visit often and have dinner together.

This _____ we will visit my _____ at her farm.

We both want to be _____ in the future.

Name

Read each sentence. Pick the word that makes sense in the sentence. Write the word on the blank line.

1. (Stir, Stare) the soup in the pot.   _____

2. The (beard, bird) built a nest in the bush.   _____

3. Mort (heart, hurt) his hand.   _____

4. It is Bert's (turn, torn) to catch the ball.   _____

5. My brother always (burns, barns) the fish.   _____

6. Deb's sister is (farm, first) in her class.   _____

7. Paula munches (hear, her) lunch in the park.   _____

8. The lush (ferns, firms) are by the window.   _____

9. There was (dart, dirt) on the kitchen floor.   _____

10. The kitten's (fur, for) was soft and long.   _____

Name

Copy the sentence that tells about each picture.

1.

Jake makes a purple cape.

Jake bakes a yellow cake.

2.

The drapes are on the table.

The grapes are on the plate.

3.

A snake is in a circus cage.

A bracelet is in the center case.

4.

The race was at my place.

The plane went into space.

5.

Her name is on the page.

Her face was on the vase.

Use a red crayon to color all the ball words that have
the long *a* sound as in **wave** and **lace**.

Name

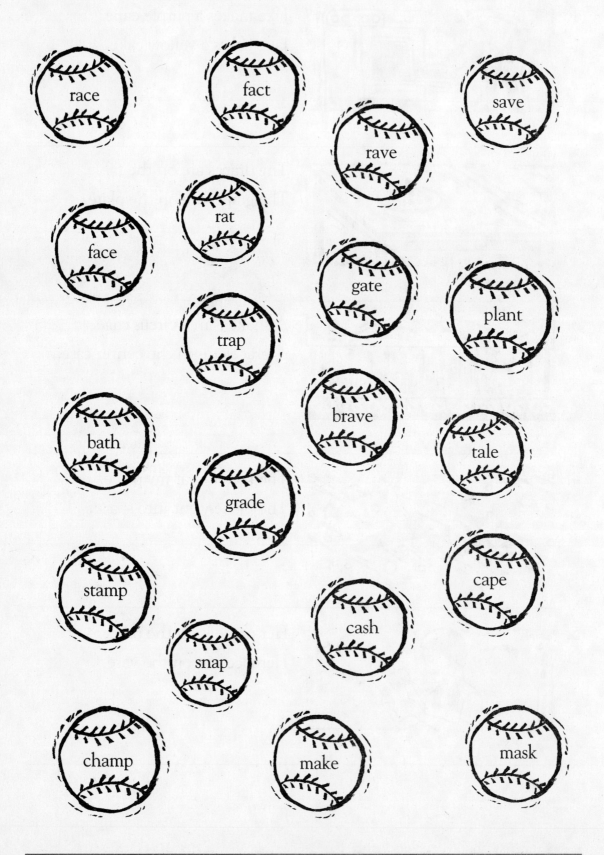

race fact save rave face rat gate plant trap brave bath tale grade stamp cape cash snap champ make mask

There are words missing in each sentence. Pick the words that make sense in the sentence. Write that word on the blank line.

1. The _____ started _____.

       gem game   late lit

2. Today we had to _____ the _____off the car windows.

       scrap scrape   ice is

3. The magician _____ on _____ in a long, black _____.

      cane came   stamp stage   cap cape

4. Dad read about the ship in _____ in the _____.

       speck space   paper pattern

5. Jo and Terry _____ cookies with animal _____.

       at ate   sharks shapes

6. My friend _____ at me when she got on the _____.

      waved washed   plan plane

7. _____ me a _____ near the _____.

   Sand Save   place plank   tab table

Name

Use a red crayon to color all the words with the **a** sound
as in **tap.**

Use a yellow crayon to color all the words with the **a**
sound as in **tape.**

Name

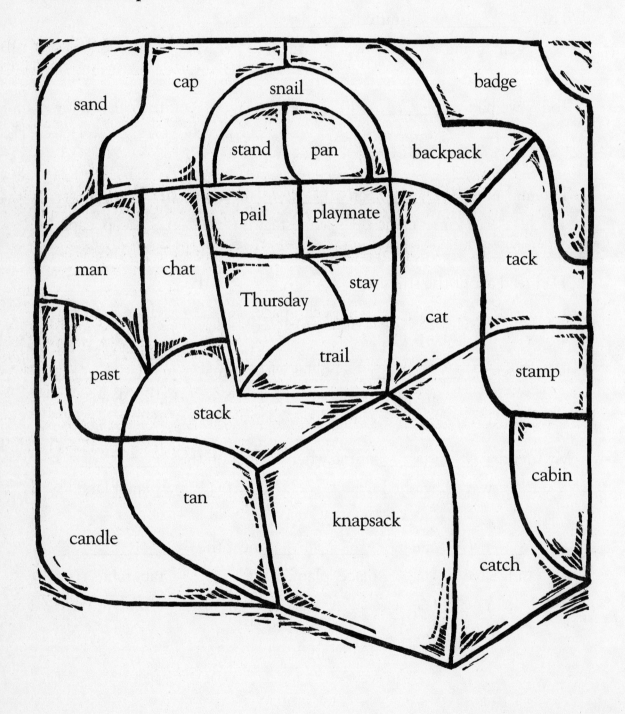

Phonics Review

Read each sentence. Look at the picture. Then, write a
word with *ai* or *ay* to complete the sentence.

1. We always have to wait for the
_____ to arrive.

2. The mayor of the city wants the
_____ delivered without fail.

3. The woman gets paid for
_____ houses.

4. Today is a _____
day in May.

5. May we _____ in the
haystacks for my birthday?

★ On another sheet of paper, write five words that are spelled with *ai* or
ay as in *pain* or *pay.*

Name

Read each clue below. Think of a word with the long *a* sound spelled with *ai* or *ay* that means the same as the clue. Write each word in the puzzle below.

ACROSS

1. to go out to sea in a ship

2. to be scared

3. another word for perhaps

DOWN

1. to remain in one place, to not go away

4. to do something for fun

5. a row of metal rings or links that are put together

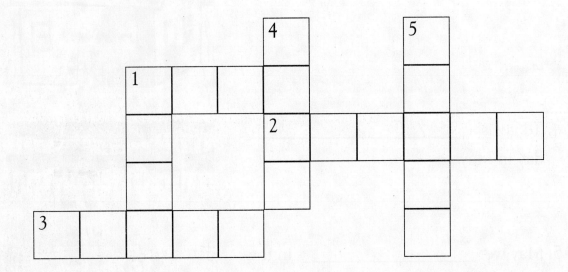

★ On another sheet of paper, write a sentence using each word in the puzzle.

Phonics Review

Draw a balloon around the words that have the *e* sound
as in *me*.

these

then

fresh   her

help
                                  we
              she   zebra

secret   chest   best

                    even
pretend

nest

Name

Use a blue crayon to color all the turtles with words that
have the long *e* sound as in **Pete.**

Phonics Review

Find the hidden picture in the box. Draw a line to connect
the dots for all the words that have the long *e* sound as in
Pete and **we.** Connect the words in ABC order.

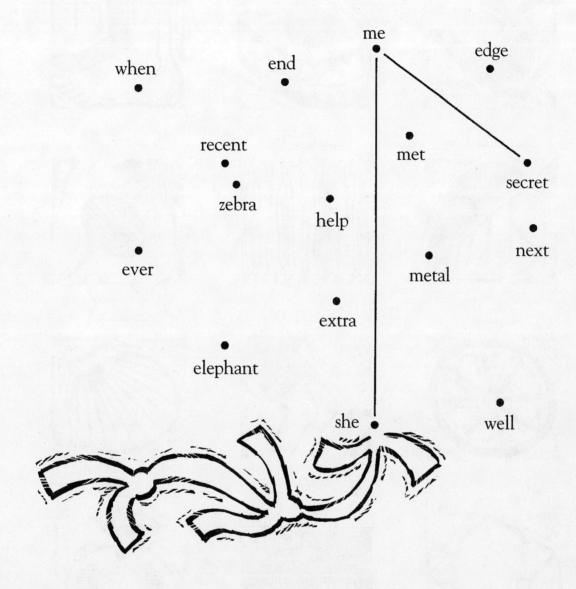

Now use some of the words with long *e* in your own sentences.

_____

_____

_____

_____

_____

Name

Fill in the blank lines with the letters that will make
each word name the picture above it.

Name

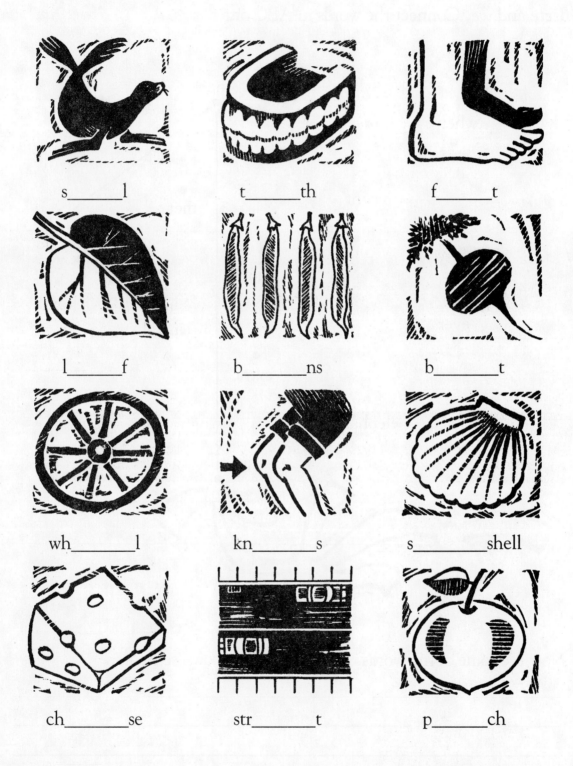

s____l   t____th   f____t

l___f   b____ns   b____t

wh____l   kn____s   s____shell

ch____se   str____t   p____ch

★ On another sheet of paper, draw a picture of the following words:
beach, meal, bee.

Look at each picture and the two words next to it. Pick the word that names the picture. Write the word on the blank line.

1.  meat

   meet

   _____

2.  feel

   feet

   _____

3.  bee

   be

   _____

4.  week

   weak

   _____

5.  it

   eat

   _____

6. tree

   treat

   _____

Name

Pick the right word for each sentence. Write the word
on the blank line.

1. I will _____ you over there.   meat
   The _____ is not well done.   meet

_____

2. Can you _____ the parade?   sea
   We picked shells by the _____.   see

_____

3. Pete and Andy had a nice _____ .   meal
   Mr. Lensky has a _____ dog.   mean

_____

4. Linda's desk is always so _____ .   need
   Joe and Vern _____ new clothes.   neat

_____

5. Save us good _____ at the show.   seeds
   We planted many _____ in our garden.   seats

_____

6. Where have you _____ all afternoon?   bean
   There was one _____ left on my plate.   been

_____

7. They went on a vacation for one _____ .   weak
   I felt _____ after running for so long.   week

_____

Phonics Review

Use a red crayon to color all the words with the short *e* sound as in *pet.*

Use a blue crayon to color all the words with the long *e* sound as in **Pete.**

felt	believe	field	friend	west
blend	pest	gremlin	grief	theft
families	never	noisy	extra	babysit
enter	bunnies	then	spend	thief
chest	pest	dent	test	ladybug

With a partner, find words in books you have read that
have the same long *e* spellings as in **baby** or **babies.**
Write the words. Then use four of the words in your
own sentences. Trade papers with your partner to
proofread each other's work.

Words

_____   _____   _____   _____

_____   _____   _____   _____

_____   _____   _____   _____

_____   _____   _____   _____

Sentences

_____

_____

_____

_____

_____

_____

_____

_____

_____

_____

_____

_____

Look at each picture. Then read the word next to it below the blank line. Change the word to mean more than one. Write the new word on the blank line.

Animals

_____
pony

_____
bunny

_____
puppy

Flowers

_____
daisy

_____
lily

_____
pansy

Now change the word below the blank line to mean only one. Write the new word on the blank line.

Things to Eat

_____
cookies

_____
candies

_____
cherries

People

_____
babies

_____
ladies

_____
families

Read each sentence. Pick the word that makes sense in
the sentence. Write the word on the blank line.

1. Mike is a brave _____.
              knit   knight

2. One _____ day, Mike _____ off to
        bright   bring   rids   rides
_____ a dragon. He is not _____.
  fight   fit   frightened   flight
But, Mike does not know that the dragon does not _____ to fight.
                                       lick   like

3. At last, Mike _____ the dragon _____ in a cave.
                fins   finds   hitting   hiding

4. "Come out and _____!" yells Mike.
                fist   fight

5. "At this _____ of _____? Come in and
            tin   time   night   nip
_____!" says the dragon.
  dine   din

6. The table is a _____! The food is quite _____!
           sit   sight   fin   fine

7. And so they eat _____ and drink water
            rich   rice
with a _____ of _____. It is such a delight!
  slice   slick   lime   lint

Name

Use a blue crayon to color all the carrots with words
that have the long *i* sound as in *spider*.

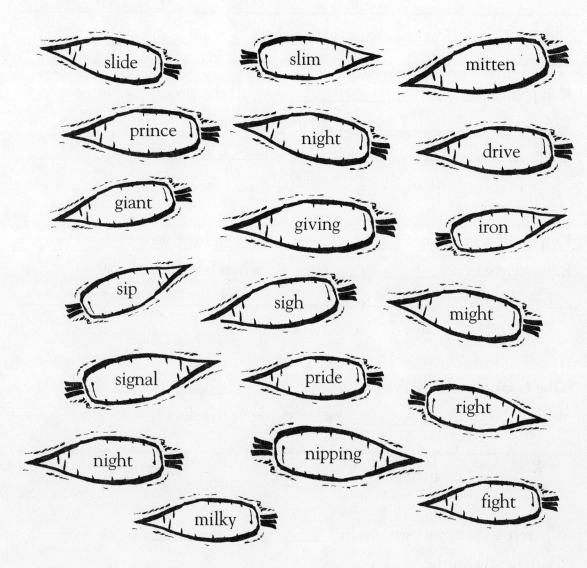

Now use some of the words you chose to write sentences
of your own.

_____

_____

_____

_____

_____

Name

Read each sentence. Pick the word that makes sense in
the sentence. Write that word on the blank line.

_____

write   right

Karen thinks she is _____ all the time.
Will you _____ to me from camp?

_____

fight   fright

Ken and Todd will not _____ anymore.
Randy gave us a _____ when he yelled at us.

_____

mine   might

That book you are reading is _____ !
Who _____ be knocking at the door?

_____

light   line

When it is dark, we turn on the _____ .
Write neatly on the _____ .

_____

bite   bright

Will took a big _____ out of his sandwich.
The sun is too _____ today.

_____

Name

Pick the word in the box that makes sense in each sentence. Write the word on the blank line.

1. I will _____ my wet feet.

   Sam _____ his feet.

| dries |
| dry |

2. Dad _____ the meat for dinner.

   Mom and Dad _____ the meat for dinner.

| fry |
| fries |

3. There are five apple _____.

   There is only one apple _____.

| pie |
| pies |

4. The little _____ cry when they are hungry.

   The little _____ cries when he is hungry.

| babies |
| baby |

5. The _____ plays all night long.

   The _____ play all night long.

| puppies |
| puppy |

6. The boy _____ very hard to learn.

   The boys _____ very hard to learn.

| try |
| tries |

Read each sentence. Pick the word that makes sense in each sentence. Write that word on the blank line.

dries   dry

1. Pete _____ the dishes every night.

    Sue will _____ the sheets in the machine.

fry   fries

2. Who _____ the meat for dinner?

    Will they _____ the chicken tonight?

spies   spy

3. Several _____ were caught by the police.

    One _____ escaped from the police.

fly   flies

4. The plane will _____ high in the sky.

    Which plane _____ the fastest?

tries   try

5. I will _____ to be there early.

    Dad _____ to make cookies for us.

cry   cries

6. The baby _____ very little.

    Don't _____ over the broken toy.

With a partner, find words in books you have read that have the same long *i* spellings as in **fly** or **flies.** Write the words. Then use four of the words in your own sentences. Trade papers with your partner to proofread each other's work.

Words

_____   _____   _____   _____

_____   _____   _____   _____

_____   _____   _____   _____

_____   _____   _____   _____

Sentences

Copyright © 1995 Open Court Publishing Company

Name

There are words with missing letters in the sentences below. Write the missing letter **o** or the letters **oe** on the blank lines to complete each word.

1. My t____s are c____ld today.

2. The n____te said that I s____ld the bike.

3. The g____ld ph____ne is in the ____ld chest.

4. Joe wr____te a p____m about a dog.

5. I saw a ph____to of a frog in a r____be.

Name

Use a red crayon to color all the cloud words that have
the long *o* sound as in **bone** or **toe**.

home

horn

shoe

dock

hoe

doe

broke

spoke

spot

fog

poke

form

phone

Now use some of the words you chose to write sentences
of your own.

_____

_____

_____

_____

_____

_____

Name

Look at each picture. Then read each sentence. Circle the word that makes sense in the sentence. Write that word on the blank line.

too   toes   tows

A foot has five _____.

tone   throws   throne

A king sits on a _____.

Zoo   Zebra   Zero

_____ comes before one.

does   dome   doe

A _____ lives in the forest.

boom   bone   born

My dog likes to play with a _____.

Some things are missing from this picture. Read the
story. Then draw the things that are missing.

1. On the kitchen table there is a yellow bowl of oatmeal.
2. A green plate of toast with jam is on the table.
3. A loaf of bread is on the stove.
4. There is a window above the sink.
5. A boy washes his hands with soap at the sink.
6. There is a snowman outside the window.

Name

Read each clue. Then write a word with long **o** as in **low** or **boat** that means the same thing as the clue. The first letter of each word is given.

1. The day after today   t_____
2. The opposite of *fast*   s_____
3. Another word for *path*   r_____
4. To become bigger   g_____
5. Bread baked in one piece   l_____
6. Something used for washing and cleaning   s_____
7. To rest on top of water   f_____
8. To go or come after   f_____

Now write a sentence using each word.

1. _____

2. _____

3. _____

4. _____

5. _____

6. _____

7. _____

8. _____

Name

The little train needs to know the names of the stations where it will stop. The names of the stations have the long **o** sound, spelled with **ow** or **oa**. With a partner, name the stations by filling in the blanks with **ow** or **oa** words. Then on another sheet of paper write a sentence using each word.

ow words	**oa** words
_____	_____
_____	_____
_____	_____
_____	_____
_____	_____
_____	_____

Name

Circle the words in the box that have the **u** sound as in *use*. Then write the words on the blank lines below.

mule   tub   huge   few

                    fun

          nut   music

                              universe

cute   hug

                    must

          cut   bugle   pew

                                              museum

          fudge   mud

                    usual

judge   fuse   sun   barbecue

_____   _____   _____

_____   _____   _____

_____   _____   _____

_____   _____   _____

Read each sentence. Circle the word that makes sense in
the sentence. Write that word on the blank line.

cut   cute

Andy has a _____ smile.

buggy   bugle

Sam played the _____ in the band.

fuel   flew

Sally will put _____ in her car.

music   mushy

The sound of _____ came from the window.

cubs   cubes

There are no more ice _____ left to put in our lemonade.

feud   few

Only a _____ children went to the zoo.

Name

Name _____

Use a red crayon to color all the football words that have the long *u* sound as in *use* and *mule.* Then use some of the long *u* words in your own sentences.

uniform

upper

human

cute

cut

united

pupil

must

music

future

huge

puppy

bugle

butter

thump

_____

_____

_____

_____

_____

_____

Copy the sentence that tells about each picture.

1. The man rides the mule.
2. The man reads the mail.

_____

3. I gave a big hug to my dog.
4. I gave a huge bone to my dog.

_____

5. The man can run and play on the path.
6. The mail came in the rain by plane.

_____

7. I bet those pets are a bat and a cat.
8. I beat those eggs to bake a cake.

_____

9. Three robbers are hiding in the tall bush.
10. The bright yellow robes are on the table.

_____

Name

Look at each picture. Circle the word that names the picture. Then finish the sentence by writing the word on the blank line.

hug

huge

Mom gives June a _____ .

note

not

Dot has a _____ from Jane.

ripe

rip

Mike has a _____ in his pants.

pine

pin

There is a _____ by the road.

tub

tube

Buy a _____ of toothpaste.

cubs

cubes

I have ice _____ in my cup.

Read each sentence. Circle the word that makes sense
in the sentence. Copy the word on the blank line.

1. I made a (sweet, swift) treat. _____

2. Fred got a (cute, cut) puppy for a pet. _____

3. I would like to fly to the (moon, moan). _____

4. My (fleet, feet) are warm in these socks. _____

5. The kittens (played, planned) with the yarn. _____

6. We (hoped, hopped) to see the show. _____

7. Ed likes to eat lean (meet, meat). _____

8. Zoos (rose, raise) all kinds of animals. _____

9. A (kit, kite) can sail in the wind. _____

10. What a (cut, cute) baby she has! _____

11. Bud plays the (bugle, boggle) in the band. _____

12. The (plan, plane) left one hour ago. _____

13. Sally (tries, try) hard to ride her bike. _____

14. Will you (write, right) to me from camp? _____

15. The children (try, tries) to be quiet. _____

Read the riddles. Find the word in the list that answers
each riddle. Write the word on the blank line.

moon   noon   zoo   moose   boot   student

scoop   truth   broom   glue   tooth   pool

1. I'm used for sweeping. _____

2. I'm used for swimming. _____

3. I come out at night. _____

4. I'm used to chew food. _____

5. I'm a big animal. _____

6. I'm worn on one foot. _____

7. I'm the middle of the day. _____

8. I go with ice cream. _____

9. I'm a place where animals live. _____

10. I make things stick together. _____

11. I'm someone in a school. _____

12. I'm what you should always tell. _____

Name

Read the riddles. Find the word in the list that answers
each riddle. Write the word on the blank line.

cruel   pool
ruler   noon
flute   chew
stew   blue

1. I am another word for *mean*. _____

2. I am a place where you can go swimming. _____

3. I am a color. _____

4. I am a musical instrument. _____

5. I am something good to eat. _____

6. I am used for measuring things. _____

7. I am the middle of the day. _____

8. I am what you do with your food. _____

Name

Circle the words in the box that have the **oo** sound as in
hoot, grew, or ***glue.*** Then write a sentence for each
word you circled.

Name

toe	threw	phone
coast clown	toast	spoon
moon	crown	due
flew		true

_____

_____

_____

_____

_____

_____

_____

_____

_____

_____ __ ___

_____

_____

_____

Read each sentence. Pick the word that makes sense in the sentence. Write the word on the blank line.

1. There is a tree by the _____.

                          brook   break

2. My mom is a _____ _____.

               got   good   cake   cook

3. There is a worm on the _____.

                   hook   hoot

4. The deer lives in the _____.

                words   woods

5. I like to read _____ about explorers.

            books   boats

6. The leaves in the trees _____ in the wind.

              shark   shook

7. She hurt her _____ when she fell.

            food   foot

Name

Read each sentence. Find the word in the box that
makes sense in the sentence. Write the word on the
blank line. Use each word only once.

hook	book	brook
shook	good	
wood	cook	foot
look	wool	

1. The leaves in the tree _____ in the wind.

2. We went to _____ at the seals in the zoo.

3. My desk is made of strong _____ .

4. Ed read a _____ about travels in space.

5. Blueberry ice cream tastes _____ .

6. My mom is a good _____ .

7. Rita's skirt is made of _____ .

8. The fish got off the_____ .

9. Vern hit the ball with his left _____ .

10. The water in the _____ is very clear.

Name

Read each sentence. Pick the word that makes sense in the sentence. Write the word on the blank line.

1. The water in the _____ was cold.
   broke brook

2. Who _____ the last sandwich?
   took tuck

3. The pirate had a _____ leg.
   wooden would

4. The _____ stole the gems.
   cork crook

5. Bobby _____ behind the door.
   stood stock

6. Steam came out of the _____ of the car.
   hood hoop

7. Dan _____ the rugs and left them in the sun.
   shack shook

Name

Pick a word from the word list to finish the sentences in the story below.

gown	town	shout	how
flowers	clown	brown	cow
crown	tower	down	downtown

1. A _____ came to _____.

2. He wore a spotted robe and a
_____ on his head.

3. He also had a bunch of fresh _____.

4. He climbed a high _____.

5. When he came _____, he had a
_____ with him. Everyone started to
_____.

6. I don't know _____ he did it!

Name

Look at each picture. Circle the word that names the picture. Then write that word on the blank line in the sentence.

crouch   crown   crowd

A _____ is worn on the head.

house   how   howl

Ben lives in a big _____.

bounce   gown   grown

The princess wore a fancy _____ to the ball.

cow   clown   cloud

That _____ looks like an animal.

blouse   blow   browse

My sister has a brown _____.

Pick a word from the list to finish the sentences.

blouses	brown	power
cows	growl	flowers
crowd	clown	clouds

1. Did the dog _____ at the prowlers?

2. I counted four _____ in her closet.

3. There is a vase without _____ on the table.

4. The _____ did not make a sound in the barn.

5. Tippy the _____ had a smiling round face.

6. Sam found a _____ puppy on the street.

7. A large _____ showed up in the town to watch the parade.

8. Last night, the _____ went off in the tower.

9. The dark _____ usually mean that it is going to rain.

Phonics Review

There are words with missing letters in the sentences below. Write the missing letters *au* or *aw* on the blank lines to finish each word.

1. A mouse was on the l____n.

2. "What should I do?" said the mouse with a y____n.

3. "Should I do my l____ndry under the f____cet?

4. Should I become an ____thor and write a book?

5. Or should I dr____ a picture instead?

6. I think I will do what I like best. I will eat

   three s_____sages with str_____berry s_____ce."

Write the word on the blank line to finish each sentence.

1. The farmer put the _____ in the barn. He _____ it slowly.

                straw slaw   hauled hopped

2. The party was on the _____. There was ice cream with

                loud lawn

   chocolate _____ .

        size sauce

3. The boys got up at _____ . They wanted to visit the _____

              dawn down   hinted haunted

   house.

4. We _____ from our work when we _____ how late it was.

   paws paused   saw sauce

5. Janice was happy because her _____ won first prize.

               drawing draining

6. The _____ _____ because she was tired.

   lawyer leaner   yawned yanked

7. The _____ uses its _____ to get its food.

     hike hawk   claws clowns

8. My dog hurt his _____ . It was my _____ .

     pause paws   found fault

Read each sentence. Look at the picture. Write a word with **aw** or **au** that matches the picture and finishes the sentence.

1. Some _____ ate plants.

2. The hawk has sharp _____ .

3. Paul had _____ for lunch.

4. Dad had to wash three loads of

_____ .

5. Why don't you _____ a picture of your house?

★ On another sheet of paper, write five words that are spelled with **aw** or **au** as in **hawk** or **sauce.**

Name

Pick a word from the list that makes sense in each
sentence. Write the word on the blank line.

noise	enjoy	toil	boys
royal	choice	soil	coil
boil	join	rejoice	toys

1. The farmer gets the _____ ready for planting.

2. The _____ are in the box.

3. Let's _____ the three _____ playing in the park.

4. _____ the potatoes and roast the meat.

5. The _____ palace has three towers.

6. That band makes too much _____!

7. Do you _____ watching films?

Pick a word from the list to finish each sentence. Write
the word on the blank line.

oil   coin   voice   boiling
royal   toys   boy   noise

1. Andy is the new _____ in our class.

2. The potatoes are _____ in the pan.

3. Marsha has a large _____ collection.

4. A queen belongs to a _____ family.

5. Alex has a beautiful _____ .

6. Pete fries the fish in _____ .

7. My brother has many _____ .

8. The cars made too much _____ .

★ On another sheet of paper, write five words that are spelled with *oi* or
oy as in *soil* or *joy*.

Name

Read each sentence. Look at the words next to each
sentence. Pick the correct word for each blank so that the
sentence makes sense. Write the words on the blanks.

_____

1. Dad _____ the meat for the _____ .

boys

broils

_____

2. Meg and Sue will really _____ the club they

   want to _____ .

join

enjoy

_____

3. We had a _____ of _____ : trains or

   planes.

choice

toys

_____

4. The _____ fruit had to be _____ .

destroyed

spoiled

_____

5. A great deal of _____ was coming out of the

   _____ palace.

noise

royal

_____

6. We _____ fish in very hot _____ .

oil

boil

_____

7. Her _____ is a _____ to listen to.

voice

joy

_____

Name

OUTLAW WORDS

a	best
after	big
again	break
am	build
an	built
and	busy
anyone	but
are	buy
as	can
ask	clothes
at	come
away	could
be	cover
bear	did
beautiful	do
berry	does

eight	he
enough	heard
every	help
eyes	her
fast	here
first	him
five	his
for	hurray
four	I
friend	if
gave	in
get	is
give	it
gone	just
great	keep
guess	laugh
had	laughter
has	like
have	little

Name

lived	out
look	pretty
love	pull
make	put
many	ran
me	ride
move	said
much	say
my	says
no	see
none	seven
not	she
nothing	shoe
of	should
off	show
oh	so
on	some
once	somewhere
one	special

that	walk
the	want
their	was
them	water
then	we
these	were
they	what
thing	when
this	where
three	which
through	who
to	why
today	will
too	with
trouble	woman
two	would
under	yes
up	you
us	your

　　　　　　　　　　　　　　　　　　　Phonics Review